WHEN GRACE FINDS YOU

SAY GOODBYE
TO PERFECTIONISM
AND FIND PEACE

FELICIA LANDIE

WHEN GRACE FINDS YOU
Copyright © 2021 by Felicia Landie

All rights reserved. Neither this publication nor any part of this publication may be reproduced or transmitted in any form or by any means, electronic or mechanical, including photocopying, recording or any information storage and retrieval system, without permission in writing from the author.

Unless otherwise indicated, Scripture quotations are taken from the Holy Bible, New Living Translation, Copyright © 1996, 2004, 2007 by Tyndale House Foundation. Used by permission of Tyndale House Publishers, Inc., Carol Stream, Illinois 60188. All rights reserved. Scripture quotations marked ESV are taken from The Holy Bible, English Standard Version, Copyright © 2001 by Crossway, a publishing ministry of Good News Publishers. Used by permission. All rights reserved. Scripture quotations marked NIV are taken from The Holy Bible, New International Version® NIV® Copyright © 1973 1978 1984 2011 by Biblica, Inc. TM Used by permission. All rights reserved worldwide.

Print ISBN: 978-1-4866-2227-6
eBook ISBN: 978-1-4866-2228-3

Word Alive Press
119 De Baets Street, Winnipeg, MB R2J 3R9
www.wordalivepress.ca

Cataloguing in Publication may be obtained through Library and Archives Canada

Advance praise for *When Grace Finds You*

This book felt like holding a mirror up to my face. I sure wish I could send a copy back in time to twenty-year-old me; it would have been a relief to know I wasn't alone. Felicia speaks so much truth in these pages—read it and know that you are good in God.

—Michelle Ott
Fellow "Good Girl"

We can easily fall into the lie of the enemy believing that God is hard to please. The truth is: the Lord generously and readily makes his saving grace available to those who would seek him through his Son. Felicia provides a well-articulated testimonial of wrestling with the Lord in Scripture over this truth. Join her on her journey of tasting the grace of the Lord who delights to readily give it to you in Christ Jesus.

—Rev. Travis Johnston
Instructor, Millar College of the Bible

As a child I was taught to say grace before a meal. We couldn't wait until grace was finished so we could eat. Felicia reminds us not to move on past grace to the meal but to taste grace. Grace is sweet. Grace is satisfying. Grace is greater than all my sins.

—Kelvin Thiessen
Director of Admissions at Millar College of the Bible

With all tact and humility, Felicia gives us a fresh look into perhaps the most foundational-yet-forgotten tenet of the Christian faith: grace. Sharing from experiences oh so familiar to any believer, Felicia speaks Biblical truth to soothe, steady, and inspire the doubting and jaded soul. *When Grace Finds You* is a beautiful reminder I'll be keeping on the nightstand where I can reach for it time and time again.

—Karis Turner
Wife, Mother, and "Grace Person" in training

This book provides a fresh look at how God relates to us, especially in the difficult personal journeys that most of us will face at one time or another. Its many stories and illustrations will keep you turning the pages. Some will make you laugh, others may bring tears, but either way, they will make you think and rethink your understanding of God's unconditional love for us all.

—Paul Chamberlain, PhD.
Professor of ethics, apologetics and leadership
Trinity Western University

To Mark—you are a gift from God, and I love you.

CONTENTS

	Introduction	ix
1.	How God Changes People	1
2.	Believing Lies	7
3.	Symptoms of Unbelief	15
4.	Saved by Grace	27
5.	Sanctified by Grace	35
6.	Gutsy Grace	41
7.	What Pain Produces	49
8.	When I Realized He Was Kind	55
9.	When I Question My Salvation	63
10.	Grace for my Body	69
11.	Grace People	77
12.	Grace Leads to Selflessness	89
13.	Let Him Love You	99
	Epilogue: Stop Working	103

INTRODUCTION

This book is for the striver, the girl who feels like she can do it all... or at least, almost. It's for the girl who knows how to please, who knows the Bible verses, the doctrine, the right answers. It's for the girl who looks put together and good to everyone else, who knows how to say the right things and do what she's told.

This book is for the worrier, the girl who looks great on the outside, but, on the inside, feels like she's never enough. Because goodness comes easily, perfection seems almost attainable, and yet she can never get there. Some days she longs for and tries to grab it for herself. But no matter how hard she tries, she can't quite get there. On good days, she asks, "Why didn't I do better?" On bad days, she feels like a failure and a disgusting human being.

This book is for the good girl who has been told all her life that she's sweet, nice, and compliant, and yet a little voice inside never gives her a break, a whisper that she's never enough. She's a wretched sinner who needs to do better. That whisper tells her, "You're not following Jesus... You know all those passages about the godly? That's not you. You are far from repentant, far from godly, far from a servant of Christ. And as for other people? They think you're gross. Don't you remember all that chocolate you ate? Your hips and arms will be wearing that for sure. Remember that girl you saw yesterday? She has it all together. If you could be like her, you'd be perfect and happy—a small body, a sweet spirit—she's got it all. Be like her... you're a loser and condemned if you don't."

This book is for the rebel who feels like she's made too many mistakes to be forgiven, like she can't forgive herself for what she's done. It's for the girl who's tried everything, who's given herself away, who's lost her innocence, her passion, her hope. She's given up her family and her youth for pleasure and licence. She's lived in the world and has come away empty. Regret clings to her, and she can't shake free.

This book is for the prodigal, the one who's wandered from home and spent everything. She thought sex, drugs, and money would make her happy. Perhaps attention and power and independence would satisfy, but now she's alone. She wonders if God could ever forgive her, if her life can ever be normal again. She feels condemned, and she believes no one will accept her.

This book is for the doubter hurt by religious people, who feels like no one understands, harbouring questions either secretly or openly. She wants to believe but can hardly bring herself to do so. She wants to trust, but her trust has been broken too many times. She thinks: *If God is anything like the Christians I know, I don't want anything to do with him.*

Whoever you are—the striver, the worrier, the good girl, the rebel, the prodigal, or the doubter—I'm thankful you picked up this book because I have something life-changing to tell you. It can be summarized in one word: grace. Have you tasted it? Notice I didn't say, have you heard of it? If anyone has stepped inside a church (or even if they haven't), they've heard of grace. But very few have *tasted* it. Some people, like myself, are on a journey of taking grace in. Think of it like a hot cup of coffee (or fill in your favourite beverage). You begin by smelling the delicious aroma. Or, perhaps, if you're lucky like me, you start your day hearing the coffee grinder in the early morning hours. The smell fills the house and entices you. You grab a mug, and with the first sip, your taste buds do a happy dance. You savour every drop, but the benefits don't stop there. The energy fills you, and you feel good and strengthened. The effects are lasting, improving your performance, attention, and interactions with others throughout your day.

I think this is how grace works. For some, they are just hearing the grinder. For others, they are smelling the aroma. Some might be taking the first sip. Some could be downing the cup. Finally, some may be living grace-fuelled lives. Usually, these steps aren't consecutive. I think we need to be constantly tasting to be living. However, if you look at your life and see a significant lack of grace, believing you're condemned rather than accepted, if you are more critical than compassionate, perhaps you need to taste more grace.

Lest you think that I've mastered this process, I want to assure you of the contrary. I'm writing truth that I naturally forget, the very message my heart needs. I am a striver, a rule follower. Grace is hard for me to believe, but it's the very thing that can transform me.

How I want to be transformed! As I think about who I want to be in ten, twenty, or thirty years, I think: gracious. Naturally, I am anxious, critical, and self-loathing. I see so many flaws in me, others, and the world. I want to be perfect, and I want the world to be perfect. When I mess up, I feel defeated and broken. I don't want to stay this way. I want to be gracious.

This is my hope for you, dear reader. While my story begins with a perfectionist, your story may begin with a prodigal, but here's the truth: we both fall short. We are both desperately needy for grace. God's standard is so high that even when prideful people like me think I can attain it, I always realize I can't. I fall flat on my face and discover my brokenness all over again. The answer for the perfectionist is the same answer for the prodigal. It's Jesus. It's grace.

For the past few months, I've been working at an addiction-recovery centre for women, and I've seen prodigals experience God's grace. I've seen loved ones taste it too. My hope is that through this book, you and I will be grace people, people who have tasted something other-worldly and been bold enough to believe it's true.

INTRODUCTION

I love grace people. When I think about the women who have influenced me the most, the people I choose to be around, or the woman I want to be, I think about grace people. I think about someone who has internalized God's grace to such an extent that it pours out of them. There is a calmness, an "I'm okay" about them, that draws me in. They live in a way that says to a watching world, "I like who I am. I'm secure. I'm free, and it's okay if I'm not perfect." Their actions declare: "I am confident in my decisions. I am not condemned, and I can enjoy life." This characteristic is appealing to me—because it is so unnatural to me.

Does it feel unnatural? Does it feel almost impossible, like wishful thinking? I want to tell you that it's not. It's not impossible because one) Jesus changes people; and, two) those women I look up to—most of them aren't naturally grace people either. They're naturally rule followers, rebels, but they've been supernaturally transformed by the one who gives them abundant life. They've been rescued from condemnation and loved beyond measure, and here's the kicker: they believe it.

Dear reader, it is my prayer that by the end of this book, we wouldn't just *know* Jesus loves us and shows us grace, but we would *believe* it. We would taste it, and, as we internalize the truth, we would become grace people.

"We know how much God loves us, and we have put our trust in his love" (1 John 4:16).

PRAYER

Jesus, I'm tired. I've carried the weight for so long. I know you are gracious, but I often see you as cruel. I know you are kind, but I often see you as harsh, mean, and condemning. I am broken. I am overwhelmed by my sin. I need your mercy, and I need to believe and trust that you love me. Help me to rest in your love. Transform me by changing the way I think. Make me a new person. Free me with your truth. Help me to stop believing lies about You, others, myself, and the world around me. I'm ready.

HOW GOD CHANGES PEOPLE

CHAPTER ONE

Remember those ladies I described earlier, the ones I admire? They are gracious today. They are grace-full, and yet they weren't always like that. In fact, they'd probably admit they still struggle to be so. However, they've grown and are growing. Though they naturally lack grace, now they are blooming with it.

One of my friends (we'll call her Kylie) didn't grow up in a Christian home. She attended Christian camp for years, and for a long time, she didn't turn to Christ. She went to camp because it was fun. There were probably cabin leaders and other staff who reached out to her and loved her. But Kylie didn't trust in Jesus. As she got older, she began to feel like camp was done. She recalls one May long weekend in her later teens. A camp contact asked, "Just come one more time." Reluctantly, she agreed, and on that weekend, something changed. Kylie doesn't remember what was said, and she can't explain it—she went to camp one person and left another. Kylie was changed forever.

Naturally, Kylie rejected Jesus. She went to camp for the fun of it. Naturally, Kylie is a rule follower. Her fallback is nothing like grace. But I don't know *that* Kylie. I'll tell you about the Kylie I do know.

The Kylie I know is not a grace-less, Jesus-less camper who just came for fun. She's not rule-obsessed or harsh. She's the camp speaker who tells dozens of elementary students that God not only loves them but likes them. She's the friend who gets me pumped with inspiration and radiates enthusiasm for life. She's the grade-two teacher who tells her students that Jesus came for everyone, whether they are parents, Walmart workers, or homeless people. She's the lady with the contagious laugh and cute house. Kylie is a grace person.

Another friend (we'll call her Marissa) is (like me) a rule-follower. You could say she gets me. She told me a story once that absolutely blew my mind. It didn't surprise me because it was a foreign concept. It didn't shock me because it was a crazy tale. It blew my mind because it was so relatable. Marissa told me about when she was dating a guy. She was at his parents' house, and she had used their bathroom. There was a bottle of lotion on the counter, and, like most people, Marissa used a bit. However, she felt incredibly guilty and thought to slide her "terrible deed" into the conversation to ease her conscience. She told her boyfriend's mom what she did, and of course, the lady was surprised and confused. Of course, she could use the lotion. That's why it was there! But Marissa had been so guilt-driven that she felt terrible about something ridiculous. This wasn't an uncommon occurrence. She felt guilty and worried about many things. "Gray issues" sent her thoughts spinning. She was so motivated to do the right thing, that she felt trapped in her own brain. Condemnation gripped her heart.

Marissa would be the first to admit that she still struggles, but she has grown in grace. She told her mom once, "I feel like I'm always going to struggle with this."

Her mom disagreed, "You don't have to." Marissa didn't have to live in constant guilt. She didn't have to listen to the "inner critic" all her life, and amazingly, she has gained so much freedom. Marissa once gave me this piece of advice. She said, "Think about how God talks. Remember a time when you knew he had spoken to you. Write it down. Go back to it." One of the biggest helps for Marissa was learning to recognize God's voice. When she felt that vague guilt, when her thoughts were spinning, or when she felt condemned, she knew it wasn't God. When she had an idea that she thought was from God, she would pray, "God, if this is you, show me in your way. If it's not, help me to forget it."

The Marissa I know isn't the guilt-driven girl who apologizes for using the bathroom lotion. She is free and confident. She enjoys life—being a mom and having a home. Marissa is a grace person.

I used to work with another lady (her name will be Jen) who wasn't a rule follower like Marissa, nor a camp junkie who didn't trust Jesus like Kylie. She was a drug dealer. While Jen grew up going to church, she ended up in a tough place. She sold and did drugs. She spent years in this life. She became well-versed in all of it, and from many people's perspectives, her life was in shambles. But then, Jen met Jesus. Her life radically changed. Like Kylie, I don't think Jen could put her finger on one specific thing. She might not be able to describe precisely how it happened, but as he does, Jesus transformed her. He broke through her darkness with his heart-softening, soul-rebirthing, life-altering grace.

The Jen I know isn't the drug dealer whose life is in ruins. She is the lady who loves the broken because she understands them. She is the woman who is so herself and comfortable being herself. She is the person who still struggles and still feels weak but who gives her life to give others hope. She has so experienced God's grace that I feel accepted, safe, and seen when around her. Jen is a grace person.

I want to tell you about one more person. Me. I'm a perfectionist who struggles with anxiety, self-loathing, and comparison. I want to do what is right but feel constantly accused. I try to look, act, and feel perfect. Some may think I'm put together, but inside, I feel condemned. When I fail or think I fail, I feel miserable.

But just the other day, a friend told me something crazy. Her words knocked my socks off. She told me how she sees me.

The Felicia she knows is not the one who feels condemned. She's the lady who holds herself to a standard of grace and encourages others to do the same. I don't say this to boast but to give hope. I am far from where I want to be. I don't always walk in grace. However, if Jesus and his gospel can change a grace-less camper, a guilt-ridden good girl, and a broken drug dealer, He can change me. I can become a grace-person, and you can, too. No matter who you are or what you've done, how broken or condemned you feel, Jesus wants you. His love and grace changes people. Are you ready to be transformed? Are you ready to be a grace person?

20 YEARS

Your eyes are still the same
They dance with blue and grey
Though a little tired
They still do love to play
Your laugh is quite endearing
It makes me chuckle too
Reminiscing on our adventures
In that 80-square-foot dorm room
So much time has passed
The years have slipped away
But now you sit before me
And I don't know what to say
Something's surely changed
I can't quite ascertain

You start to speak, and it confirms
You're just not quite the same
Your heart is bigger yet more firm
It rests more than it runs
Your love is deeper and sincere
But you still sure can have fun
The love of Jesus shines right through
Your words and acts are sweet
While you were nice so long ago
Your love is now complete
For now, you trust that God loves you
Now you've quit your fight
Now you know His grace so free
And it truly is a sight
God's grace indeed has changed you
It's such a marvelous feat
You're still my sweet and dear old friend
But now you've been set free

PRAYER

Jesus, I don't want to stay the same. I want to really believe—believe that you are gracious and kind and that you love me. Forgive me for not believing those things. Help me to rest in your finished work. Help me to trust that when you said, "It is finished," you meant it.

BELIEVING LIES

CHAPTER TWO

I was homeschooled for a lot of my growing-up years. From Kindergarten through Grade 10, I learned at home. Overall, I enjoyed it. I loved the flexibility and chance to get creative. I loved using my imagination and having so much time to play. Some days, I would pack my backpack and pretend I was walking to class. Other days, I would put on my pioneer garb and head off to a make-believe one-room schoolhouse. Sometimes my sisters would set up our little easel and be my teachers, but this always meant they had to do their work in the afternoons (aka I was sadly stuck playing by myself).

One interesting opportunity was taking online classes. Our school board provided online courses in which we could read and discuss classic literature, practice our creative writing, or learn a bit of Latin. I enjoyed these classes (I know... I'm a bit of a nerd). Despite my enthusiasm for Jane Austen and deep discussions, I had some struggles.

Even then, I feared being bad and dishonest. I was terrified that I'd miss a word or phrase in my assigned reading and then be lying in saying I'd read the whole book. Or worse, I wouldn't really have completed the course, and in years to come (maybe even on my wedding day), I'd be haunted by the accusation of being a fraud. When this belief is fleshed out, you can hear how ridiculous it sounds. However, my fear was real, and it led me to a strange sort of obsession. It would take me forever to read books, constantly repeating what I read. Whether I told my mom about this or she simply caught on, she set out to help me. She would have me read aloud to her, and if I started repeating words or phrases, she would alert me.

This may seem like a silly example, but it was an early symptom of my predicament. It was an indicator of the fear lodged within me.

I was afraid of getting it wrong because I felt I'd be condemned if I did.

I remember other times when this fear would arise. I would be at my childhood friend's house, enjoying a snack, and I would accidentally get a few crumbs on the ground. I would frantically try to clean them, even though they were hardly visible to the naked eye,. While most people wouldn't think twice, I did. I felt compelled to apologize for the littlest things to quiet my guilt.

My friend found this rather humorous, and I now agree that it is. But it's also sad.

In many areas, I felt compelled to over-explain, over-apologize, and over-examine. I know God has made me conscientious, and He loves honesty. However, my actions indicate a deeper issue, a fear that held me captive. I didn't want to live in bondage or be obsessive, yet I felt enslaved to being correct. It wasn't a healthy desire to serve God. It was an unreasonable fear of punishment.

When I felt guilty about the possibility of not reading a word or phrase or about getting crumbs on my friend's floor, I assumed the guilt was God-given. Or I just acted like it was, without thinking critically about it.

When I examine my guilty feelings, I often realize they are vague. My guilt is often more inspired by questions than statements. Here are some examples:

"What if you are sinning?"

"What if you aren't being obedient?"

"What if you're not really a Christian?"

At times when I'm reading Scripture, I'll get a vague sense of guilt. I'll read a verse like, *"For the LORD watches over the path of the godly, but the path of the wicked leads to destruction"* (Psalm 1:6), and I will hear, "You're not really godly. You identify more with the wicked."

This guilt is vague and unhelpful. Sometimes, it's just a straight-out lie, coming out of a false sense of identity.

While I still mess up, that isn't who I am. I'm not one of the wicked; I'm one of the godly.

The problem with believing a false identity is that it's not only a lie—it leads to more lies. If I don't believe the truth of who I am, I can't read the Bible correctly. The Bible awards the righteous and condemns sinners.

When I believe that my fundamental identity is wicked, I'm not fully resting in the gospel.

God made us good. He made us in His image. However, when the serpent tempted Eve, she and the whole human race fell. They became broken and entirely sinful. They became wicked.

However, that isn't the end of the story. We couldn't save ourselves or earn God's approval, so Jesus came to do it for us. Jesus met the standard by not only living perfectly, He received the punishment we deserve. If we receive this amazing gift, not only is our sin forgiven—Jesus's perfect record becomes ours. We are in Christ. When the Father looks at us, He sees Jesus. He sees a perfect record. He sees godliness.

Our identity is joined to Christ's. No longer are we "the lost," "wretched sinners," or "the wicked." We are "the righteous."

Once we rest in who we are *already*, we can be propelled forward to follow Jesus. We can read verses about God blessing the righteous and say, "Jesus, thank you for blessing me. Thank you that I am yours forever, and you have given me so much! Now, help me to live righteously more and more."

Our fundamental identity is secure, and all that is left is to live it out.

What keeps us from resting in this truth? While I just spelled out the truth in black and white, I struggle to believe it on a daily basis. Why?

It's because there is a liar and an accuser.

"When he lies, it is consistent with his character; for he is a liar and the father of lies" (John 8:44b).

"For the accuser of our brothers and sisters has been thrown down to earth— the one who accuses them before our God day and night" (Rev. 12:10b).

The liar and accuser is alive and working. While we are safe in our salvation, Satan wants to trip us up. He wants to make us ineffective, and one way he tries to do this is by lying to us.

Now the thing about lies—bear with me—is that they sound like the truth. A lie wouldn't be effective if it were obviously untrue.

Effective lies sound a lot like truth. They could be mostly false with bits of truth sprinkled in. Or they could be mostly true with some lies sprinkled in. The truth could just be twisted.

When Satan met Eve in the garden, he sought to deceive her. He questioned what God had said, asking, *"Did God really say you must not eat the fruit from any of the trees in the garden"* (Genesis 3:1b).

Even his opening question twists the truth, trying to get her to doubt God's words ("did he *really*..."). He then stealthily switches a word or two ("the fruit from *any* of the trees").

At first, Eve did pretty well. She corrected the serpent and repeated what God actually said.

Then the serpent lied directly, saying she wouldn't die and adding, *"God knows that your eyes will be opened as soon as you eat it, and you will be like God, knowing both good and evil"* (Genesis 3:5).

Then Eve gave in.

I fear punishment when I start believing lies, doubting that I am saved by grace. I stop believing that salvation is a gift that I can't earn. I stop believing that I am safe in God's hand. I stop believing that God saves me and sanctifies me. I start believing that I must pay him back, keep myself in his hand, and make myself holy by human effort.

Gracelessness is disbelieving the gospel that sets me free, and thus I find myself in bondage.

IT'S WHAT HE DOES

He lies. He twists. It's what he does
His words sound so like truth
He whispers doubts, inspires fear
Determined to confuse

"You're not good or safe or loved."
"Your sin is far too great."
"You've done too much and gone too far."
"For you it's far too late."

As you believe the lies he tells.
You feel chained in defeat
But if you rest yourself in truth
You'll finally be free.

PRAYER

God, forgive me for believing lies. Help me to believe the truth about who you are and who I am in you.

SYMPTOMS OF UNBELIEF

CHAPTER THREE

I have seen many symptoms of unbelief in myself. When I don't believe the love God has for me, it manifests and reveals itself in many ways.

1. DECISION PARALYSIS

One of the symptoms is decision paralysis. Decisions are hard. I struggle to make choices because I fear making the wrong ones. This fear is wrong because I tend to believe I'll be condemned if I mess up.

Rather than seeing a forgiving Father, I see God as a harsh taskmaster. I see the Christian life as a tightrope—one wrong move, and I'm done. I see my journey with Christ not as a narrow path of sacrifice fuelled by joy but a ledge where I'm one step away from wrath and condemnation. I forget about forgiveness.

Decisions come, and sometimes we'll choose wrongly. Sometimes neither option is wrong, and we are free to choose either. But no matter what, we are secure in God's hand and can find forgiveness at his feet.

2. DEPENDING ON OTHERS TO MAKE MY DECISIONS

Another symptom of unbelief is depending on others to make decisions. If I can somehow transfer the responsibility, perhaps I can also shift the blame. How terrible... how rooted in unbelief.

Our fear doesn't reveal a lack of love on God's part. Instead, it shows a lack of belief in His love.

> *God is love, and all who live in love live in God, and God lives in them. And as we live in God, our love grows more perfect. So we will not be afraid on the day of judgment, but we can face him with confidence because we live like Jesus here in this world. Such love has no fear because perfect love expels all fear. If we are afraid, it is for fear of punishment, and this shows that we have not fully experienced his perfect love. We love each other because he loved us first.*
>
> —1 John 4:16b–19

Did you catch that? As we fully experience God's love, we lose fear. We lose the fear of judgment because we genuinely *believe* that he loves and pardons us and gives us his perfect righteousness. God's love produces fruit. It produces confidence and love in us for others.

When I depend on others to make decisions, I don't believe in God's love. I'm unloving towards others, trying to cast the responsibility on them, so I can avoid the blame if needed. How unloving! How opposite to the life God has for me! Fear is, indeed, a love problem.

3. OVER-APOLOGIZING

Another symptom of my unbelief is over-apologizing. Rather than trusting that Jesus declares me righteous, I try to make myself feel good through others. Rather than apologizing out of love for another, or even a healthy conscience, I apologize to comfort myself. Rather than listening to the Holy Spirit's whisper, I soothe internal accusations my own way.

Over-apologizing is also unloving to others. In my case, it is rooted in unbelief in the finished work of Jesus, an attempt to make myself good rather than leave that to Jesus.

4. SELF-CONDEMNATION

When we don't receive his grace that covers our sin, with what are we left? Condemnation. We see our sin, but we don't see our Saviour. Without a Saviour to forgive and declare us righteous, we are rightly condemned.

Left in condemnation, we see our hearts filled with pride, unbelief, and rebellion, and we feel doomed. We see our broken world, and we feel condemned for not doing anything about it. We see our bodies with eyes of disgust, pressured to change, and we feel rotten for not living up to some arbitrary standard of beauty.

Without a Saviour, we either try to work hard to make ourselves acceptable, or we become a prodigal. Either way, we run. We run from Jesus, the only Saviour.

5. OBSESSIONS

When I was in a particularly dark year, one verse that meant a lot was Isaiah 26:3. It says, *"You will keep in perfect peace all who trust in you, all whose thoughts are fixed on you!"* Unbelief says we are alone. Grace says that we have a caring Father who welcomes us, carries us and gives us peace when life is hard and doesn't make sense.

I often believe that understanding brings peace, and to a certain extent, that's true. The more we understand what Jesus has done for us and who he is, we will find more reasons to be at peace.

However, it isn't always that . For one thing, just because I know something in my head doesn't mean I'll believe it in my heart. Additionally, even if I find one answer to one question, soon there'll be another problem to solve. If we believe that understanding is our source of peace, it will always be out-of-reach.

My mom once described her relationship with my dad this way: as they got to know each other in the beginning, and as their relationship has continued, she has grown to "trust his heart." She knows who he is and trusts him so that, even when she doesn't understand his actions, or even when his actions frustrate her, she is at peace and believes the best about him. She knows that he genuinely wants to follow Jesus, serve others, and do right, so her heart is secure. Her mind can rest because she isn't wondering, "Is he going to leave me? Is he doing me harm? Is he just in it for himself? Is he walking away from his faith?"

When we know someone's heart, we have confidence in them.

And here's the kicker. My mom can trust my dad a lot. We can really trust our friends to be there for us, but there is always a chance that they will fail.

God never will. When things aren't black and white, when answers evade us, we can have complete confidence in our Lord because we "know His heart."

6. BINGE EATING

I think one reason I've struggled with binge eating is that it's my attempt to get off the tightrope. When I do something I consider a "failure" (like overeating), I experience God's grace. This approach isn't the right way to experience grace. We shouldn't "sin that grace abounds." But sometimes, I get so tired of trying to be perfect that I purposely fall to feel free.

7. ZONING OUT

A life without grace is hard. It brings depression, anxiety, and fear. It's hopeless because I can never justify myself. Without a Saviour, I'm left to care for myself, and I'm not strong enough for such a task.

Therefore, what can a graceless person do to ease the pain and weight of unbelief? Zone out. Ignore reality. Try to take their mind off their fears. While this may seem to work temporarily, it leaves people emptier than before.

I have tried to deal with my gracelessness and unbelief in many ways. I've tried to run from my fears, but what if... for just a moment... we imagined a life where this absence of grace was unnecessary? What if we believed that God loved us and showed us love by giving us what we don't deserve? We wouldn't need to run, zone out, ignore, or try to take our minds off our feelings. Rather, we could live out of heartfelt peace, believing that we are declared righteous, forgiven, and safe.

8. BRITTLE RELATIONSHIPS

When I'm not resting in God's grace, I don't have grace for others. Relationships become brittle. Imagine a wooden bridge suspended over water. It might handle a little weight but put a little pressure on it, and it snaps. There's no give, no wiggle room, no flexibility. If there's a hint of a problem, it cracks like a twig in a fire pit. Rather than being made of strong elastic, relationships become more like uncooked spaghetti noodles or old rubber bands.

I can unknowingly transfer my fear of condemnation onto another, and that affects my interactions with others. Rather than believing in God's grace for me and others, I believe that one wrong move will shatter any hope of a relationship. If one little thing goes wrong, the whole thing should be thrown out.

When we are "grace-less," there isn't room for imperfections. We either blind ourselves to our sin or feel destroyed by it, and when others act in ways we don't like (whether sinful or not), we get frustrated at best and condemning at worst.

Jesus put it this way. When describing a certain woman, he said, *"I tell you, her sins—and they are many—have been forgiven, so she has shown me much love. But a person who is forgiven little shows only little love"* (Luke 7:47).

May we never forget the weight of our sin and the sufficiency of our Saviour. We did nothing to earn it. He has forgiven us of much, and this enables us to have gracious hearts towards others.

9. WHAT IF IT'S AN IDOL?

Sometimes I think I need to understand every sin in my heart so *I* can make it right. While we have a responsibility to pursue sanctification, I can become proud in my ability to fix myself. I believe that if I can understand my sin, I can make it right. Perhaps *this* is my idolatry—thinking I can get right with God on my own, worshipping myself... believing I'm self-sufficient.

Rather than trusting in my own ability, I want to echo David.

"How can I know all the sins lurking in my heart? Cleanse me from these hidden faults" (Psalm 19:12).

10. FEAR OF SPIRITUAL AUTHORITY

I am usually comfortable asking for help, insight, and wisdom. However, sometimes this can go too far.

When I meet someone who seems really "spiritual," I quickly assume what they would think and how they would speak into my life. I question how God has led me. I question what other godly mentors have said. I doubt my own ability to make decisions. I become consumed with fear of what "they" would say. I either resent them, fear them, or ask them their opinion. Sometimes I do all the above, and do you know what? They often aren't as hard on me as I am. They often speak truths that I have heard before. My heart is often lighter, and I feel relieved—that is until I meet another really "spiritual" person to whom I attach an assumed opinion. I fear making the wrong decisions. I fear what others might think.

Rather than trusting Jesus's acceptance and guidance, I look to others to make me feel *okay*.

11. STRUGGLING TO RECEIVE GIFTS

My mom once told me, "Felicia, I think you're more willing to receive hard things from God than good things." She was right. It sounds crazy, and before you think I'm a sucker for punishment, let me tell you, I hate loneliness. I like getting what I want. I desire happiness and pleasure just as much as the next person.

But when faced with a good thing—or a choice—I tend to believe that the harder thing is the holier thing, which isn't always the case. Sometimes it takes more faith to receive a good thing than a hard thing. At least when it's hard, I can feel like I'm earning brownie points or stars in a heavenly contest.

Sometimes, Christmas is hard. I think of the people who go without, who don't have a place to stay, family to love, or gifts to unwrap. I struggle to enjoy the holidays even though it's hands-down my favourite time of year. I feel I need to earn some of the good things I experience. Perhaps if I care for someone enough or sacrifice something I enjoy, I could feel better about receiving a good thing. However, when I think I can work hard enough to deserve something, that is pride—because I don't deserve anything good.

12. ANXIETY

I have experienced anxiety about many things, a lot of which stems from perfectionism. My counsellor helped me see this. She said, "Felicia, you are chasing the god of perfection instead of the perfect God." When I feel anxious about work, I'm often worried about what people will think or if I'll be able to do what's asked. I want to be liked and capable so badly that it gives me anxiety. I want to be perfect, a perfect Christian, a perfect employee and co-worker, a perfect wife and friend—all while looking and feeling perfect. That sounds like a recipe for anxiety.

Unbelief has many symptoms. When I don't believe the truth, my heart isn't at rest. Instead of Jesus leading me, I become enslaved to fear, condemnation, and doubt.

But it doesn't have to be this way...

THE TIGHTROPE

> Careful, careful, walk it slow
> You could fall, don't you know?
> One wrong move, one misstep
> Sends you hurling to your death.
> Gently, lightly, no mistakes
> Keep it nice; keep it fake.
> God will judge you if you fall
> If you slip, you'll lose it all

Balance, balance, eyes ahead
Wear your mask, or you're dead
Obey demands; try to please
Earn your place; earn your peace.
Then I slip; then I crash
Down I fall with a splash
I'm condemned; I've done it now!
Secret sins are shouted loud.
I tried perfection, but missed the mark
I walked the tightrope but broke my heart
But as I cry and swim to shore
I hear you whisper, "Child, there's more."
"You thought you'd make it way up there.
"Believing I neither knew nor cared.
"But let me tell you something true.
"Let me tell you some good news."
"You don't have to earn your keep.
You don't have to walk or leap.
You don't have to meet the standard.
Because *I've* done it with flying colours."
"Get in my arms; get on my back.
"Know I love you, and that is that.
"Don't climb up there; just look at me.
"Believe my words, and you'll be free."

PRAYER

God, cleanse me of my unbelief. I choose to trust that you are gracious and have done the work to save me. Help me walk in that freedom.

SAVED BY GRACE
CHAPTER FOUR

The answer to these symptoms of unbelief is a precious gift. The gift is that we can be saved from condemnation and the wrath that we fear—we can stop trying to earn acceptance and be welcomed into a family. Here is the gift, dear reader. Reach out and take it.

I remember the best Christmas gift I ever received. I'd been dreaming about the *American Girl* dolls for a while. I poured over the magazines filled with beautiful dolls, doll clothing, and accessories. As much as I wanted a doll, I didn't think I would get one. It wasn't on my radar. My sisters teamed together, and when they presented me with the big box, I didn't even suspect what it would be. However, as I unwrapped the present and was confronted with the familiar logo, I went ballistic. As I opened it further, I found that it wasn't just one but TWO dolls. They were twin baby dolls, and I couldn't be happier. I danced around the room and fearlessly showed my delight. I was the happiest girl alive.

I had my dolls sleep under the Christmas tree that night. I affectionately named them Chloe Dawn and Ethan John (Dawn after my middle name and John after my dad's name). I still have the dolls packed away to this day. They are treasures.

We've been given a gift that surpasses any earthly treasure—salvation. God saved us by sending Jesus to live the perfect life in our place, to take our condemnation through his death, and to rise again, showing that it's done!

This gift is for anyone, whoever they may be... whatever they have done. It's for hardened criminals, and it's for children. And it's for everyone in between.

Amy has been in jail. While she grew up Catholic, she got into a bad way. She became an addict and got into crime, and then she got into prison.

Amy had a hard life and made some bad choices. She had to learn to be tough.

But God's grace changed her.

Today, Amy is warm and bubbly, with an infectious joy that can only be attributed to Jesus's powerful work. She's still on a journey towards healing, but she is making progress. She's an encouragement to others and a ray of sunshine. With tattooed arms, bleached hair, crazy manicured nails, and a contagious laugh, Amy speaks openly about Jesus.

But all isn't sunshine and roses. Amy struggles to forgive herself. Or perhaps she struggles to accept God's forgiveness. Either way, she sometimes feels weighed down by her past. She is still in contact with some friends from jail, and she told me about one lady in particular. This lady had been Amy's roommate, and she was fairly religious. She and Amy had grown close, and Amy cared for her but was concerned. You see, the lady had killed someone, and Amy asked her friend with the most genuine care and concern, "Do you think you're going to heaven?"

"I don't know," was her friend's response. "I hope so."

Amy now looked at me. She was worried. Amy loves Jesus, but she didn't know the extent of God's grace.

Well, I had the privilege of telling her, "Amy, if your friend truly puts her faith in Jesus, she can go to Heaven." I told her about the thief on the cross to whom Jesus said, *"Today, you will be with me in paradise"* (Luke 23:43).

I got to share the most radically freeing fact with her—anyone who comes to Jesus can be saved, even a murderer.

God can save anyone. His grace is that big.

People tend to think that what they did is too big. "Surely God couldn't forgive all that." We can believe that our sin is too terrible for God to make right. We can believe we're too messed up, too gross, too broken.

Amy may have felt like that. Her friend may have too.

But it's not just criminals who struggle to accept God's forgiveness.

It can be little camp kids... like me.

I remember attending Bible camp as a kid. I went a few summers and had a blast. I would always attend with my best friend, and we were pretty shy until we got comfortable with people. I remember we had two cabin leaders who we just thought the world of. Their camp nicknames were Espresso and Bubbles. Espresso was the cool, quiet type with pretty, blonde hair. She was a little more serious and subdued but so sweet. Bubbles was a little more fun-loving, as her name implies. She was light-hearted but still had depth. She was friendly and warm. My friend and I fell in love with these ladies. They were cool, but even cooler, they acted like we were.

I remember feeling worried that week. Oh, I loved the camp culture, the meals, crafts, chapels, cabin time, tuck time, and though intimidating, I didn't mind the group games. However, one night I was worried. I remembered something I had done years before, something that wasn't good. I felt guilty, scared, and it was eating away at my conscience.

I remember sitting out in the main square with Espresso. We sat on a log, side by side, the stylish, subdued, and sweet cabin leader and the scrawny, shy, and sorry camper.

I must've told her that I wanted to talk. She knew something was on my mind, but I didn't go into detail. I told her of a past mistake, something I felt terrible about. She didn't press for specifics or hound me for more than I wanted to share. She listened. My little ten-year-old self was torn up. I was anxious with a heavy conscience. *How could I have done such a thing?*

When I finished, I remember Espresso telling me of God's grace. She told me about a song, a song that explained how God deals with our sin. He removes it as far as the east is from the west. He forgives—it's gone.

I think Espresso wrote me a letter that week also, quoting Bible verses. Espresso was one of the first people I remember who taught me God's grace. Other than my parents, she was one of the first people to help me apply the gospel. While my heart was bleeding with guilt and fear, she applied the ointment of God's mercy.

What's funny is that Espresso probably doesn't remember this. I think I saw her years later, and she might not have even recognized me (it's been at least ten years). But I remember. I remember how God used her that night, sitting beside me on that log. That surreal moment is etched in my memory. Espresso was one of the first grace people who touched my life. She probably didn't think much of the encounter. I don't know. She probably had tons of campers that summer and maybe other summers besides, but that night was special for me.

It's not just criminals who need God's mercy and grace but struggle to accept it—it's everyone. Everyone has bleeding wounds of guilt and fear. Everyone needs to be reminded of the truth: God's mercy is big enough to handle their sin, for He removes their sin as far as the east is the from the west.

Whether you're a tough criminal or a troubled camper, or someone in between, God's grace is big enough. You don't have to carry your sin anymore. If you ask Him, Jesus will remove it. He will cast it away. Jesus died so that your punishment can be applied to Him. You can go free.

Here's the gift. Reach out and take it.

TISSUE PAPER

I feel the crinkly paper.
The gift then comes in sight.
I stop and wonder filled with doubt
Will I do this right?
What if I tear the paper?
Or ruin the pretty bag?
What if I go too quickly?
What if I start to lag?
"Just take the gift my darling one."
Take the gift of my Son.
I lift the wrapping back
And gaze to see what's there
Then in dread I turn and gasp
What if it needs repair?
What if it's not what I asked for?
What if it's somehow cracked?
What if I don't really want it?

Maybe you should take it back.
"Just take the gift my darling one."
Take the gift of my Son.
I finally get to look inside.
It's more lovely than I thought.
Fear wells in me once again
Surely this should be bought.
I reach into my nearby purse
My offer now prepared.
Let me pay or work for you
I need this to be fair.
You pull me close and soothe my fear.
You tell me it's okay
Open your hands and take it all.
My love is here to stay.
I give you good beyond your dreams.
I give what money can't buy
It's time that you believed my love.
And told your doubts goodbye

PRAYER

Jesus, thank you for your gift of salvation. You lived, died, and rose, and I am not condemned. Thank you that I have your perfect record. I did nothing to earn it. Help me to rest here.

PRAYER IF YOU DON'T KNOW JESUS

Lord, I am so broken. My sin is so big, and I can't fix it. I know that you did everything for me. I know that you lived the perfect life I couldn't, died the death I deserve and came back to life. Save me. I turn to you. Rescue me. Have mercy on me and forgive me.

SANCTIFIED BY GRACE
CHAPTER FIVE

Growing up in the church, I heard a lot about accepting Jesus. I heard the gospel invitation to receive Christ. From an early age, I could have told you how Jesus died on the cross for my sins and rose again. I could have told you that people need to believe in Jesus to be saved. However, my understanding of salvation—of grace—wasn't nearly extensive enough. Somehow amid gospel presentations, altar calls, and raising your hand to accept Jesus, I missed what happens next. I started believing that once saved, it was practically up to us to grow. People have to do the four *main tasks* (i.e. read the Bible, pray, go to church, and tell others about Jesus). And, they were basically on their own, and it's all up to them to succeed.

This is what I believed. Satan cunningly deceived and even twisted scripture to paralyze me like the serpent in the garden or Jesus's temptation in the desert,. He mixes truth like "Reading your Bible is good" or "Pray without ceasing" and adds lies like, "If you don't, you're condemned" or "It's all on you." In the end, it's just a mess.

My mind quickly tires of dissecting truth from error, and I am left trying to calm my anxious mind and free my burdened heart.

There was a church in Bible times that was similarly deceived. The Galatian church started by believing the good news that saved them, but then they added to this—grace itself was no longer sufficient for salvation or spiritual growth. But the gospel says that Jesus not only graciously rescues us from sin's punishment, He also graciously enables us to live for Him. The fact that I can't perfect myself is the reason I need a Saviour. My desire for perfection is only fulfilled by the only One who is perfect.

"For by that one offering he forever made perfect those who are being made holy" (Heb. 10:14).

When Jesus died on the cross, He perfected us. It's done. In His eyes, we are without a single fault, and our growth in holiness is something that He accomplishes, not us.

If you're like me, you're wriggling in your chair, trying to make sense of all the verses that call us to live a certain way. Don't we have any responsibility?

Our responsibility has always been the same, dear reader.

Jesus told them, *"This is the only work God wants from you: Believe in the one he has sent"* (Jn. 6:29).

"So I live in this earthly body by trusting in the Son of God, who loved me and gave himself for me" (Gal. 2:20b).

Every action we do is an overflow of what Christ has already done for us. Rather than reading our Bibles and praying to earn or keep our standing with Jesus, we live out of what's already been accomplished. This may seem like a subtle switch, but it changes everything.

A lot of "Christian" actions can be done without faith. I can read my Bible, pray, and go to church very well without faith. I can be motivated by fear, condemnation, and anxiety, and that is far from living for God.

When we rest in Jesus's finished work for us and accept His gracious gift, we will want to and be able to live for him. He is committed to our sanctification. He will do it (1 Thessalonians 5:23–24)!

I think living by faith can sometimes mean watching Netflix or having a nap or hanging out with friends or literally doing anything from a place of rest in what Jesus has done.

I'm all for reading our Bibles and praying, but it must come from faith, resting in what Jesus has already done.

Leave the sanctification to God. Trust Him.

STOP LISTENING

She picks up her Bible to read about Him
Then she's flooded with guilt and deceived

"God is displeased. He's says you're out."
"You are condemned, unloved, unclean."
That's not Holy Spirit
That's not your good King
That's a bully, a fraud
Stop Listening
Hungry she walks—to get some lunch
But fear of man ensues
"Don't eat too much. They'll think you're fat."
"Your plate determines value."
That's not Holy Spirit
That's not your good King
That's a bully, a fraud
Stop Listening
She picks up her phone to text that boy
But panic begins to rise.
"You best read more and pray for days."
"If you dare enjoy those kind brown eyes."
That's not Holy Spirit
That's not your good King
That's a bully, a fraud
Stop Listening
Have you heard God's voice? Listen to Him.
His words are kinder and true
He calls you beloved—holy and good.
He sees you as spotless and new.

PRAYER

God, thank you that you will sanctify me. Thank you that you are making me holy. Thank you that I can seek to live for you as an overflow of all that you've done for me. Help me live for you, not to try to earn your love but because I already have it. Help me to stop listening to the voice of the bully that says it's all on me or I can never please you. Thank you that I am your child, and you are producing good fruit in my life.

GUTSY GRACE

CHAPTER SIX

Have you ever met someone passionate about grace? Someone strong in their conviction that God is good and kind? Someone who's walked through fire and come out realizing that what God requires of us is more freeing than they ever thought possible?

When we fear condemnation or feel tied up in indecision or burnt out by striving, it's time for gutsy grace. These fears or struggles usually begin with "What if...," or, "How dare you...."

What if I make the wrong decision about what movie to watch? What if it's inappropriate?

How dare you eat that chocolate?

What if I made this person angry by being too assertive?

I won't go on, but you get the idea. The answer to all of this is gutsy grace. Grace isn't a fluffy, feel-good rom-com type of feeling. Although it brings peace, graciousness is a characteristic of the strong. Paul prays for the Ephesians that they would have inner strength. Why? So that Christ would live in their hearts and their roots would grow deep into his love. He wanted them to be firmly rooted in Jesus and His love—and that takes strength.

As believers, we need to look fear in the eye and say along with Paul in Ephesians 2:4, *"But God."* We need to stand firm on what Christ has done for us and resist the devil's schemes.

Paul did this well.

When he writes in 2 Corinthians, he is defending his authority, claiming, *"Those who say they belong to Christ must recognize that we belong to Christ as much as they do"* (2 Corinthians 10:7). When people discredited Paul and his ministry, he didn't shirk back. He didn't give in to fear and say, "You're probably right. I shouldn't do ministry."

Paul was confident in who He was in Christ. He was confident in the work God had given him. He was gutsy.

Paul knew his sin, and he knew his Saviour. He wouldn't let anyone question the work God had given him to do.

It's a good thing Paul was confident, for he had to trailblaze new territory, reaching many Gentiles for Christ, and stand before people who knew his evil past. Paul was one of the most influential Christians in history. He wrote scripture, and he proclaimed the truth of the gospel to many Gentiles.

But he wouldn't have done these things if he hadn't been 100% convinced that God would do what He said. If

Paul had believed the lie that he was condemned for his past sin, or if he listened to those who criticized his ministry, none of the other stuff would've been possible.

Another guy with gutsy grace is David, the king of Israel. He was also a great sinner. He stole a guy's wife and then killed him. David had a terrible past but trusted his Saviour. He didn't listen to those who wrongfully accused him. Whatever their accusations, he knew the truth of what he had done, what he hadn't done, and where his heart was at. He didn't cower under others' criticisms. He knew that God would *"not constantly accuse"* (Psalm 103:9a), and he rejected others' false words.

He says, *"May those curses become the Lord's punishment for my accusers who speak evil of me"* (Psalm 109:20).

David turns the curse back on them!

Even when David knew he had sinned, he believed wholeheartedly in God's forgiveness. He writes, *"He has removed our sins as far from us as the east is from the west"* (Psalm 103:12). Additionally, after David sinned with Bathsheba, he says, *"Purify me from my sins, and I will be clean; wash me, and I will be whiter than snow"* (Psalm 53:7).

David knew he had sinned. He called out for God's mercy, but then he *knew*—if God purified him, he would be whiter than white. He was confident about grace.

I wonder, are we gutsy like Paul and David?

Gutsy grace is long overdue. It's time to stop being passionate about everything else while being beaten up by our accuser. It's time to throw down the anchor and say, "I refuse to believe the lie." Dear one, God has saved you by his grace. Let's get tougher skin.

When we read scripture or hear a message, we may feel overwhelmed by our need. When we feel the weight of our sin, it can be easy to believe we're condemned as a result because without Jesus, we are! If we don't have the right view of our sin, we'll either deny our penalty, deny our sin altogether, or wallow in feelings of condemnation.

None of these coping strategies are in line with the gospel.

So, what is the proper response to seeing my sin?

It's three words. *Yes, but God.* We need to start saying these words to ourselves and be gutsy about it.

"Yes, I sometimes struggle with having right priorities, but God."

"Yes, I sometimes have impure thoughts, but God."

"Yes, I sometimes am proud, but God."

We aren't destined for wrath any longer, so we don't have to deny sin's punishment. We're not enslaved to sin anymore, so we don't have to deny its existence. We're not condemned any longer, so we don't have to wallow in fear and shame.

Yes, we still sin, but that isn't our identity.

Yes, we still sin, but we're not destined for wrath.

Yes, we still sin, but we're not condemned or enslaved.

Yes, we still sin, but Jesus has come.

This is the truth. Let's be gutsy about it.

Gutsy Grace

I want to tell you about someone who epitomizes gutsy grace. We'll call her Lisa. Lisa is a matter-of-fact person. She is tough and discerning and can say it like it is. But Lisa also enjoys life. She has a contagious laugh that carries far and wide. I've often shared with Lisa my struggles with anxiety. I've been open with her, and she's listened a lot, showing me sympathy and kindness.

But Lisa isn't just sweet. She's gutsy.

She knows who Jesus is and what His voice sounds like. She knows the spiritual battle we're in, and she knows that our enemy is real. She knows that he tries to deceive.

I was talking with her on a particularly hard day a few months ago, sharing about the voice in my head. I told her the doubts, fears, and anxieties in my mind and heart. After I shared with her the thoughts that were swirling in my mind, she told me point blank, "That's Satan."

She knew God's voice, His gracious, truth-filled voice, and she recognized when the accuser spoke. She didn't mull his words over or give Satan the time of day. She didn't spend time questioning what she already knew was true. She just looked me straight in the eye and broke the news: I was listening to the enemy. I was believing lies.

Friends, it's time to stop believing lies. It's time for gutsy grace.

THAT GRACE GIRL

She is fiery. That grace girl.
She laughs with contagious glee.
While others are timid, unsure, and afraid
She is fearlessly free.
She is courageous. That grace girl.
When the enemy comes to accuse
When he tells her lies and feeds her fear
She stands her ground on truth.
She is strong. That grace girl.
Though her heart feels anxious and weak
Though her mind finds reasons to fear tomorrow.
She trusts the Prince of Peace.
She is lovely. That grace girl.
Her eyes are deep yet pure.
They tell the stories of darkest hours.
Where Jesus drew her near.

PRAYER

God, help me to be bold. Empower me to fight like a warrior. Help me hold up the shield of faith when doubts and fears fly in. Guard my thoughts with your salvation. Protect my heart with the knowledge of your imputed righteousness. Let the truth be what holds me up and holds me together. Enable me to be ready to share the gospel and enjoy the peace it brings. Strengthen me to fight with your Word and on my knees in my prayer. May I not be quickly shaken.

WHAT PAIN PRODUCES

CHAPTER SEVEN

Do you ever just feel "sad?"

Pain is like pressure. It squeezes tightly. You feel the discomfort, and if we run from it or resist it, we might grow bitter or feel empty. But if we let pain do what God wants it to do, what comes out of us could be something beautiful... it could be grace.

I want to be a gracious person, someone who takes the pressure off myself and frees others from the loads they carry. But sometimes, the only way to become that person is through pain. When we experience pain, we get stripped of self-sufficiency and pride, realizing just how needy we are. Yet, when sadness bears down, beautiful things can flow out.

Pain can release an aroma of grace. Tears may pour from our painful wounds, but those tears can produce compassion. We develop hearts of compassion. We can see others walking through pain and say, "I've been there, too. I get it."

However, if we don't allow ourselves to be weak, we will be less patient with others' weaknesses. They might not be vulnerable with us because they think we're put together or simply untrustworthy. Why would they want to open up to someone fake or who hasn't experienced their sorrows? When we deny pain or run from it, we lose intimacy with others.

Now, I'm not saying we wallow in it or seek it. I'm also not saying I have this figured out or mastered. I struggle to feel pain. I think it's perfectly fine to seek help and strength through godly means. It's okay to find coping mechanisms (if they are healthy). It's even okay to permit yourself to veg when you're sad. However, I don't believe it's right to deny your pain. We need to take our sorrows to God even when it's hard to find the words.

When I think of who I want to be in ten or twenty years, I think of someone gracious, strong, comfortable in their own skin, compassionate, and firm. However, the people I know who display these traits are people who have walked through pain. They have gone through fires. They have been broken and healed. Perhaps my pain is a reason to praise Jesus! Perhaps he is making me into someone beautiful, a person birthed in the fire.

When I think of people like this, I think of my mom. She is beautiful. She is okay being imperfect. She is strong, and her heart is anchored. But she wasn't always that way. I remember her telling me stories of when she was a girl. She was so insecure. Her family would have guests over, and my mom would go into her room and cry because she felt 'less than.' She didn't feel beautiful, and she struggled in many ways. Over the years, she's wrestled with fear and loneliness. She's cried and stayed awake many nights in sorrow. However, in those times, she went to the Father. She allowed the light of his grace to shine through her broken pieces and touch her heart, holding onto Jesus, even as He has held tighter onto her. Pain alone doesn't bring about lovely things, but God can use pain to make us beautiful if we let him.

Through pain, God takes us deep. We can experience intimacy with him that we wouldn't have otherwise. We can learn to recognize his kind voice.

And He is kind.

No matter the storm you're in, He is holding you.

Dear friend, if you have cried alone into your pillow, if you have felt that dark cloud over your soul, if you feel ashamed, I want to tell you about my Friend. He is not only full of truth, He is also full of grace, and that chaotic voice in your head, that dark cloud of despair, that cycle of shame, fear, and anxiety, that's not Him.

Those "what if's," obsessions, fears of the future, black holes, mental storms, and lies that say you're disgusting and condemned... that's not Him.

Those hamster wheels, spinning thoughts, that voice that says God is out to get you, the uncertainty and back and forth... that's not Him.

Do you know what He's like?

He's gracious.

And as you experience the storm with Jesus, do you know what you're becoming?

As you suffer, as you press on, oh friend, He's making something beautiful and strong. He's making a grace person out of you.

CRUSHED

You push me down
The pressure grows
Stress within me
I'm down so low
Out flow tears
Salty streams
Heart and eyes
My pain is seen
Sadness crushes
It squeezes tight
Tension rises
I want to fight
Out flows blood
Bitter wounds
Where are you God?
Anger looms
Burdens weigh
It feels titanic
My world is clouded

My thoughts then panic
    Out flows grace
      For a friend.
    I can tell them.
    "I understand."
  For while the burden
    Crushed me down
      It was His love
    That He poured out
      While the rains
      Did flow so heavy
      He was there
    To keep me steady
      I didn't see
    He stood beside
  As He crushed me
His arms stretched wide
So when you're crushed
 He's up to something
  You'll feel His heart
  And hear Him sing
 When you're crushed
  His grace will flow
 And you will bloom
 And you will grow

PRAYER

God, life is so hard. I'm tired, and I feel anxious. My heart is often sad, and sometimes, I just feel so weak. Meet me here. Hold me. I can't do this anymore. I can't do this alone. Rescue me, and bring me out the other side more at rest and confident in you. Use my tears to make me grow, and use my pain to minister to others in pain.

WHEN I REALIZED HE WAS KIND

CHAPTER EIGHT

When you think of who God is, what comes to mind? What are His character traits? You might say loving, holy, or just. You might think of the time He calmed the storm and declare, "He is powerful!" You might recall the times He healed people, opening blind eyes, making the lame walk and cleansing the lepers, and you could say honestly, "He's compassionate!"

You might think back to the Old Testament when God gave the law, and you might feel some fear. You might say He's vast, wrathful, and jealous. One could recall when God made the world and label God as creative and wise. The Psalms tell us God is near and sees everything.

When you think of God, what words come to mind? Who is He?

Every word mentioned above is true. He *is* loving, holy, just, powerful, compassionate, vast, wrathful, jealous, creative, wise, near, and omniscient. I would have used these words to describe God for many years, and I still would.

But I've also gotten a fresh picture, a new word that I'd never really dwelt upon, a word that changed me.

God is kind.

I don't know your reaction to that statement. Some of you might roll your eyes and say, "Duh!" Others may lean in, curious, and perhaps a few of you might feel tears well in your eyes. Some—and I've often fallen into this camp—might worry about a word like this. You might think, "Don't go overboard. Yes, God is kind, but He's also just!"

I've thought this. There is a fear in me of taking God's love for granted. There is a fear that if I swing too far towards His kindness, I might start excusing sin. Paul is clear that that is possible (as I alluded to earlier). However, those who do, don't understand God's grace and kindness.

When Jesus encountered broken people, He showed incredible kindness. Luke 18:35-43 describes the story of a blind beggar who heard that Jesus was passing by. The beggar knew he needed Jesus. He probably struggled and sought help all his life and experienced terrible suffering. When the beggar heard that Jesus was near, he cried out, *"Jesus, Son of David, have mercy on me"* (Luke 18:38). He was desperate. People hushed him, but he called out again, louder, *"Son of David, have mercy on me"* (Luke 18: 39).

Jesus stopped and had the man brought to Him, asking him what he wanted. The man was straightforward and to the point, *"Lord,"* he said, *"I want to see"* (Luke 18:41).

Did Jesus question his sincerity or ask for payment? Did he ask the man, "Do you think you're worthy?" Or tell him, "Buddy, it's great that you know I'm merciful, but remember... I'm also just!" No way. I picture him crouching down in front of the guy, looking into his glazed-over eyes, and, brimming with kindness, saying, *"All right, receive your sight! Your faith has healed you"* (Luke 18:42).

Jesus knew the man's heart. This broken man had one request, "Heal me," and Jesus had only one answer, "All right."

As soon as he could see, he started following Jesus, praising God, and causing others to praise Him (Luke 18:43). Does that sound like he went back to his sin? No, it sounds like sanctification. It sounds like a life pleasing to God!

We can't over-emphasize God's kindness. I don't believe we need to seek a "balance" between justice and kindness. God isn't fifty percent just and fifty percent kind. That sounds like one would cancel out the other, and we would be left stuck in our sins.

The gospel says that God is both one hundred percent just and kind. He punished one hundred percent of my sin when Jesus hung on the tree. I received one hundred percent of His mercy and kindness. In my blindness and wretchedness, I called out, "Save me," and in his mercy, he replied, "I will."

When we truly understand God's kindness, we experience freedom.

Sometimes if I feel myself getting too attached to a person or thing, I start to fear. I feel I should back away. I easily believe my love needs taming, and my joy needs to be subdued.

But is this the way God calls us to live?

Does God pull His love away from us? Does He limit His joy so that it's polite and proper?

That is not the God I know.

God's love is far from polite and proper. The Bible says He is *"rich in mercy"* (Eph. 2:4) and *"filled with unfailing love"* (Ps. 145:8). The English Standard Bible tells us that God is *"abounding in steadfast love"* (Psalm 145:8, ESV).

Love and fear don't mix. Love drives out fear. It shouldn't be the other way around.

Sure, sometimes we need to cut things out of our lives if they cause us to sin. But too often, I live in fear. I fear believing that God really loves me as much as He says. I fear accepting others and letting myself love them—loving people risks getting hurt, but that is how God made us.

When it comes to loving God and others, we need to amp things up. God never meant for us to tame our love fearfully. He never meant for us to push others away.

God's love knows no bounds.

"See what great love the Father has lavished on us, that we should be called children of God!" (1 John 3:1, NIV)

Lavish means to pour out, smother with or shower. God is not just rich in love, but He is rich in kindness and grace.

"He is so rich in kindness and grace that he purchased our freedom with the blood of his Son and forgave our sins." (Ephesians 1:7, NIV)

Friend, don't try to tame His kindness or box in His love. Don't be so afraid of making a mistake that you pull away from God or others.

You see, the enemy doesn't want us in good relationships. He doesn't want us to obey God, loving Him and others. He doesn't want us to have the abundant life that Jesus came to bring, so what does he do? For some people, he gets them caught up in adultery, murder, and lies. For others, he gets them caught up in fear. If they are afraid enough, they won't step out. They won't put their weight on Jesus, trusting that His love will hold them up.

Don't try to tame God's kindness. Don't diminish it.

When we truly believe that God is kind, we will transform. We will change from being fearful, self-condemning strivers to being wildly kind, intensely strong, deeply rooted, and unapologetically free men and women. We will be grace people.

YOUR COLOURS

I pick up my brush to paint your likeness
I open my bottles of paint
I'm certain I know your colours
Confident with no restraint
But as I start to work

I hear a voice speak low
It whispers softly, saying, "You've got
So much more to know."
"You're weary under loads of care
Your brow is furrowed still
Paint me bigger, wider, bolder
The canvas I must fill."
So I paint him bigger.
Then I paint him strong
He's mightier than I thought he was
His power reaches long
The voice returns once more and says
"You move so quick with fear
Paint me kinder, softer, gentler
I'm the One who draws you near."
So I paint him kinder
Shades of mercy I then add
He's more gentle than I ever dreamed
He lifts my burden and makes me glad
I'm done my sketch and hand it to Him
He smiles with a fatherly glow
"I'll treasure this," he says to me
"And there's even more to know."
I turn from my play and look in his eye
His strength shines bright and clear
But as I tremble in its rays
He whispers, "Daughter, have no fear."
"I'll serve you always and change the world.

I'll bear the burden bravely."
He shakes His head and lifts my chin
"You've dropped your gaze from me."
"I'm big, so do not worry.
I'm kind, so don't be afraid.
Look at me and be transformed.
You're safe and being re-made.
He spun me towards his own canvas.
A masterpiece it will be
"Hand me that brush, sweet daughter of mine."
At peace, I do it with glee.

PRAYER

God, thank you that you are kind. Thank you that you are over-the-top kind. Thank you that all my punishment has been put on Jesus. All the wrath reserved for me has been poured on Him. Thank you that I am not condemned. Thank you that you lavish your love and kindness on me, and You give me not only salvation but so many other gifts. Help me to see you for who you are. Forgive me for trying to tame your kindness or deny your love. I open my hands and receive.

WHEN I QUESTION MY SALVATION

CHAPTER NiNE

At one time or another, many believers will struggle with the assurance of their salvation. I have come to realize that believing in God's grace is also the solution to this problem.

I was in junior high when I decided to get baptized. It was a difficult decision. Looking back, it seems odd, but decisions have always been tough. I wondered if I was doing the right thing, but when I learned that baptism was an act of obedience, I decided to obey. I attended a class or two, wrote my testimony, and on Pentecost Sunday, I stood up before my church family and declared I would follow Jesus. My sweet youth pastor (I'll talk more about him later) asked me a question or two and then dunked me under.

It was done. It was beautiful.

However, people often experience testing after baptism. This was true for me. While I initially questioned if I should go through with it, I questioned if I was really saved after I got baptized. Here's what happened.

I accepted Jesus into my heart when I was three. Hence, I hardly remembered doing it. After I was baptized and had made this bold commitment, Satan started casting doubt into my mind. Had I really accepted Jesus? Had I prayed the "right prayer" (as if there is a magic formula)?

As a little girl, I had prayed many times to accept Jesus. I would pray then forget I had prayed, so I would pray again. One time, it seemed to "stick," and I felt assurance for a decade. However, now as a tween or early teen, I began praying and re-praying again—I doubted that it "worked." My deepest fear was that I wasn't truly saved, and it ate me up inside.

One day, I came across Romans 10:9.

"If you openly declare that Jesus is Lord and believe in your heart that God raised him from the dead, you will be saved" (Romans 10:9).

There it was in black and white, and there I was... doing what I would have to spend a lifetime doing—choosing to believe the truth over my feelings. I prayed something like, "God, I declare that Jesus is Lord, and I believe in my heart that you raised Him from the dead."

I obeyed the verse, and I stood on the truth.

What's funny is that I still look back to when I was three as the time that I accepted Jesus.

Throughout my life, I've continued to struggle with doubts about my salvation. I am aware of my sin and brokenness, challenging that I'm truly saved. When I read in the Bible about the godly, I think, "That's not me. How can that be me? How can I truly be saved?"

My problem lies in two areas, and for both issues, God's grace is the answer.

My first problem is that I don't believe God calls me righteous. I don't believe that when I read about "the godly," I can replace it with my name.

But I can. In God's sight, I'm godly. I'm blameless and righteous. That's not pride. It's humility—none of that's my earning. None of that's what I deserve, but all of it is true. When I don't believe God calls me righteous, it's because I think it's up to me to earn my title, and I know I fall short. It's pride in disguise because I'm still believing or at least hoping I can earn God's favour.

No wonder I lose assurance. If salvation were based on performance, no one would be able to rest easy. Because I sin every day, I would lose assurance every day.

My second problem is that I evaluate my sanctification based on emotions.

If I'm not trusting my performance, I'm trusting my feelings. Neither is trusting Christ and his grace.

I've had some wonderful mentors over the last few years. Sarah (we'll call her) was one of them. She was a thinker through and through. While I can be loaded down and tossed by my emotions, Sarah was logical. She could tell it to me straight, and she did. I am so thankful for her influence. We continue to meet when we can, and she is a good friend. I remember her telling me something once, and it stuck with me. She said something like, "Felicia, don't base your standing with God on your feelings."

In other words, don't evaluate where you're at spiritually based on your current feelings.

It's amazing to meet people who aren't feelers. They think, and they act. Rather than worrying if they feel Him, they just believe God's there. I think feelings are beautiful and God-given gifts, and we *can* feel God at times—He wants us to feel Him and experience a range of emotions. We "feelers" can learn from those who are more analytical (and vice versa). When we don't feel God, we can choose to believe what we know is true... that He's still there.

Because Jesus gave us a priceless gift, we are saved and always will be.

> *I give them eternal life, and they will never perish. No one can snatch them away from me, for my Father has given them to me, and he is more powerful than anyone else. No one can snatch them from the Father's hand. The Father and I are one.*
>
> —John 10:28-30

We are secure in God's hand. If you have turned to Him, He sees you without a fault (Eph. 1:4). He is growing you and producing fruit in you. One day, He will bring you into His presence and banish sin forever. If you're saved, you're always saved.

Trusting in my performance or emotions to tell me where I'm at with God is foolish because I'm a sinner and quickly deceived (Jer. 17:9). Rather, as I did at fourteen, I need to lay all my weight on Christ.

One more thing...

When we struggle with assurance, we need to look at the fruit of our lives. If you are God's child, God's Spirit lives in you and is producing fruit. Look at the fruit He is producing, and if you struggle to see it, ask someone who knows you and knows Jesus. Ask what they see. God says we can evaluate others based on their fruitfulness (Matt. 7:16), so listen to those who know you. Are they encouraging you with the fruit they are seeing? If they are telling you that they see fruit, stop listening to your deceptive heart.

We don't need to wonder if we're saved. We can finally rest.

Believe that God calls you good, be sharpened by other believers. When your heart condemns you, when Satan tries to accuse you, you don't have to believe it.

SAFE

Harder, faster, keep it up
Run the race or you're done
You must perform to keep his love
Pray the prayer no time for fun
Perhaps your sin is far too great
What if you have lost your place?
Perhaps you're not his child at all

What if you have slipped from grace?
Darling, you don't have to worry
Rather rest in his strong hand
Since he's mightier than every pow'r
Ever in his hand, you'll last
Lay your worries down at his feet
With his Spirit, you have been marked
Cast your cares upon him now
For He Himself lives in your heart

PRAYER

God, I praise you that you're more powerful than anything. You hold me in your hand, and no one can snatch me away. Forgive me for doubting your Word. Forgive me for trusting in my performance and feelings to tell me what's true. Fill me with assurance.

GRACE FOR MY BODY
CHAPTER TEN

For years I tried to perfect my body. Growing up, I was one of the lanky kids, with long arms, long legs, long hair, and I wore baggy jeans and loose t-shirts leftover from Vacation Bible School. I put my hair in a low ponytail, swore off makeup, and called it good.

I called it good.

I believed I knew what was good, pushing against anyone who told me otherwise. My older sisters tried to no avail to get me to buy skinny jeans. My friends loved makeup and talking about boys, but to me, that was just sinful.

I thought I knew what was good.

Enter puberty. My body started to change, and with it, my idea of what I thought was good. All of a sudden, baggy jeans, low ponytail, and VBS t-shirts didn't cut it. I became hyper-aware of how I looked, and I was uncomfortable with it. I adjusted my wardrobe to make me feel secure and beautiful.

I wanted to look good.

I watched my siblings get into fitness, and I started following Youtubers who posted workouts and "healthy eating tips." I started exercising, and slowly, I became obsessed with my appearance. I remember nights standing in the bathroom searching the web on "How to lose weight." I felt... less than.

Episodes of binge eating were part of my struggle. I was self-conscious about my body, yet I loved food. I remember trying on graduation dresses and feeling so bad about myself. My "problem areas" felt like mountains of defeat.

I wanted to feel good.

When I went to university, I enjoyed being in a running club and having a workout buddy. I felt like food was less of an issue because I was busy, happy, and had less say about what I ate or when I ate. I enjoyed cool friendships, and I often ate in groups, making binging less likely or tempting.

I felt good.

I decided not to return to university the following year, and looking back, I see God's guidance in that. However, I began to believe a lie about God. Perhaps I had entertained it before, but now, it enslaved me. I believed the lie that God was out to make my life miserable. I equated obedience with the worst possible thing I could imagine doing, and I felt captive to my feelings and thoughts. What did I do? I tried to escape. I tried to numb my heart, distract my mind, and drown out what I thought God was saying to me. How did I do this? I watched a lot of YouTube videos, and I ate...

a lot. I gained a bit of weight, and I became the heaviest I'd ever been.

I felt bad.

That was the darkest time of my life, and I've often associated gaining weight with such brokenness. Although I've healed immensely, that year reinforced the lie that skinny was spiritual and fat was sinful.

I still struggle. I don't always have a great relationship with my body or food. I sometimes struggle to view God correctly. I can idolize my weight, believing lies about God and numbing out with food and entertainment.

But...

I also am being transformed by the gospel. God's Word is settling deeper and deeper into my heart, and the truth is setting me free.

Because of Jesus, I am good, and my body is good.

This is why...

Once upon a time, there was a beautiful garden. There were fruit trees and flowers. Ducks quacked. Wolves howled. Horses whinnied in the breeze. The sun shone in the day, and the crickets sang at night. It was a wonderful garden, but God wasn't done creating. He'd made a lot of good things. The trees were good. The flowers were good. The ducks, wolves, horses, and crickets were good. The sunshine and the moon were also good.

Now, he was going to make something very good. He was going to make a person. He had an idea—something in His imagination. He was excited, ready to get started.

He gathered what He needed, a handful or two of dust. He got to sculpting, first the torso, then the arms and legs. He made the head with two eyes, one nose, one mouth. He fashioned the ears, fingers and toes.

When all was ready, He drew a deep breath. Exhaling, He watched it come to life. It was a man. It was very good.

He loved the man, and the man loved Him, but the man needed a friend.

"Go to sleep," He said.

Taking a rib from the man's body, He created again. This time, He stretched and twisted and molded, first the torso, then the arms and legs. He made the head with two eyes, one nose, and one mouth. He fashioned the ears, fingers, and toes.

When all was ready, He drew a deep breath. Exhaling, He watched it come to life. It was a woman. It was very good.

He loved the woman, and the woman loved Him.

It wasn't long before something bad happened. God's good creation, the man and woman, disobeyed Him. Suddenly, the world broke. The flowers had weeds. The wolves were wild, and the sun was hot and burned their skin. Their bodies hurt. Their hearts hurt, and they felt aware, shamefully aware and uncomfortable—they didn't see themselves as very good, as how God created them.

They tried to fix it. They tried to deal with the problem on their own. "I feel ashamed of who I am," said Eve. "Let's make clothes to cover up our brokenness. We'll make ourselves feel better."

Adam grabbed some leaves, and they got to sewing. They made some clothes and put them on. They itched, but they were the newest fashions. For a moment, they made them feel "okay."

But then they heard God's footsteps. "Did you disobey me? Did you listen to the liar instead of the One who called you very good?"

Adam and Eve were ashamed again. Even with their leaf shirts and pants made of greenery, they felt naked all over again. They felt bad. Their broken bodies reminded them of their broken souls, the sin that they chose instead of their best friend.

"Will you let me fix it?" God asked.

Adam and Eve looked at each other, wondering what would happen next. What was God up to? They couldn't guess.

Quickly, God rounded up an animal, killed it, and clothed them from its skin.

The blood stank. The sight was brutal, but God was fixing the problem. The sacrifice covered their shame.

Though they had been created very good, their sin broke them, making them ashamed. When they had seen their bodies, it was like they were looking at their dirty hearts. They felt, saw, heard, smelled, and tasted their sin—and they ran.

But God. He provided a sacrifice *to make them good again*. He covered their naked bodies *to make them good again*. When He looked at them and saw they were covered with something good—He saw them as good again.

Friends, this is the gospel.

God created us very good.

But because of sin, we became broken.

But God provided a sacrifice to make us good again. Now, He sees us without fault.

"He has reconciled you to himself through the death of Christ in his physical body. As a result, he has brought you into his own presence, and you are holy and blameless as you stand before him without a single fault" (Colossians 1:22).

Trusting in Jesus means we stop sewing fig leaves. Our shame has already been covered.

We stop trying to hide our shame behind a perfect body.

We stop trying to down our shame in a gallon of ice cream.

We stop trying to disguise our shame with perfect religion and performance.

We stop trying to hide our shame because it's already been dealt with.

We can stand tall no matter our jean size, acne, weight, workout routine or diet. We can dance, rest, and laugh because when God looks at us, He sees Jesus's perfect righteousness. We are loved, accepted, and very good in His eyes.

GOOD

You want to be good and crave perfection.
But the mirror keeps accusing you.
So you run and lift and crunch and burn.
Your fear you seek to soothe.
You want to be good and crave perfection.
But the scale is harsh and mean.
So you try to curb your hunger pains.
Believing skinny means free.
You want to be good and crave perfection.
But your sin shows otherwise.
So you strive to be a holy saint.
But you're just left breathless and dry.
You want to be good and crave perfection.
But neither can you achieve.
Rest in Him who calls you good.
You're perfect. Now be free.

PRAYER

Father, forgive me for trying to earn my acceptance through being perfect and looking perfect. Thank you for calling me good and making me perfect. Help me rest in that.

GRACE PEOPLE
CHAPTER ELEVEN

Sometimes I struggle to believe or understand how God loves me, but then He puts people in my life to show me He does. These people proclaim the gospel and share God's love without saying a word.

One lady who showed me this grace was an employer. She had three little kids, and I worked as their nanny. We'll call this lady Molly. Molly is naturally a rule-follower, a black-and-white thinker, and a high achiever. But contrary to what some might believe, being in her home helped me experience God's grace. Yes, Molly was somewhat of a perfectionist, but her home was beautiful and full of glimpses of kindness.

I remember when I would first arrive at her home. Upon ringing the doorbell, sometimes one or two of her kids would come running. Molly would answer, and I was immediately swept up into the fast-moving, life-filled energy that a family with three kids under seven brings. Molly's home was beautiful and aesthetically pleasing. She and her husband were renovating different parts of their home, doing little projects here and there. Molly managed to have a home that was kid-friendly yet also lovely to behold. It was peaceful and personal because they had touched every part. Her daughter's room could be girly and quaint, while her basement was filled with toys and blanket forts.

Her kids loved reading books. One we often read was *The Jesus Storybook Bible*. Can I just say: this book ministered to my soul!? Every story pointed to Jesus, the Rescuer, the One who could really, truly save me and make everything better. This was the message that my broken spirit longed for. My thirst for grace, my thirst for Jesus, was quenched as I read about Him in every story. As the kids and I sat on the couch, reading book after book, they would climb about, placing their chubby little hands on my arm or lap. They would get comfortable and lean against me and get lost in the story. There's nothing like a child's love to soothe a broken heart, making life suddenly good, and I could see Jesus for who He is: kind.

My running buddies in university also showed me God's grace. The group ran twice a week, and when I found out they ran through the winter, I was a little shocked. *Do people actually do that?* However, being a part of this group was probably the highlight of my year. I would run with them at least once a week, usually Tuesday mornings. I'd bundle up and get out nice and early. We would run in the neighbourhood and sometimes downtown. They pushed me to be active and go farther, but there was also so much grace. The leader of the group was usually out ahead. She was tall and fast and fit. Some people might lag, but everyone usually had a buddy.

I remember the conversations we had while we ran. They were always so uplifting and joy-filled. As our endorphins flowed, my heart was encouraged. These people loved Jesus, and they were steady. They didn't try to impress each other. They were so real, and as we ran together, a bond grew.

These people were beautiful, yet not in the flashy sense. They were healthy, pure, and full of light.

Like many of the ladies I've mentioned already, they were "radiant." That's really the best way to describe them. Of course, they had their differences. A few were music majors. One or two were English pros. Some were more subdued and serious. Some were bubbling brooks of joy, and yet, they all were grace-filled. They were kind, accepting, warm, and solid in their faith.

While they probably didn't know it, those upperclassman runners gave this young freshman a taste of grace. They showed me how good God is. In times of doubt, I can look back to people like them, recalling those days and believe that God truly loves me.

Monica is a grace lady. She's a women's dean at a Bible school, and she is one of the kindest souls I know. She sees people. She really sees them. Now, she may not notice your new hairstyle or clothing choices, but she knows if you're having a bad day. Her intuition is intact.

Monica has shown me grace. She's been through pain and disappointment, but God has taken her deep—she can tell others how beautiful and trustworthy He is. She works with young lady leaders and has an incredible ability to model grace to the "good girls." She shows them a different way. She points them to Jesus when they can so quickly look to themselves.

Monica doesn't have it all together, but she has an ability to rest in God's grace that is contagious.

Ella is another woman who exudes God's grace. When I look at her, I see someone at rest. Her work can be overwhelming and heart-wrenching. She counsels women struggling with addiction. She hears so many stories, sees so much pain, and speaks into such tragic situations. Sometimes she has to speak in court or exit women from their recovery program. She comes face to face with sin, pain, and brokenness.

And yet... Ella is also a woman at rest. I see that in her every day, a certain confidence, joy, and lightness about her. She knows how to speak her mind and listen closely. She knows how to be involved in people's lives while not getting destroyed by their pain. How does she not get overwhelmed? How does she not feel responsible to fix all of this? How is she so at rest?

It's Jesus. Ella begins every day with rest. She grabs a cup of coffee, walks out on her porch, and is still. Ella doesn't have to earn her rest. She simply receives it.

Tina and Fran were two grace ladies I knew growing up. They led a youth ministry I was a part of. Tina and Fran were two peas in a pod. They were kind, hilarious, and didn't care what people thought of them. They loved Jesus so much, and they had a freedom and joy that was contagious.

Tina was a mom of many. She and her husband lived down the street, and I remember seeing Tina often sitting on her front porch enjoying the sunshine or evening air. She was a children's ministry director, and she gave her life to love others, but she did it from a place of joyful rest in Christ.

Fran was a mom of one. She drove a cool, red Rav-4, and she liked to work out. She had a great laugh, and she embraced life without holding back. She worked at a school dining hall, and she shone in all she did.

Tina and Fran weren't perfect. While I never knew a lot about them, their walks with Jesus never felt unattainable. They were normal, living everyday lives, laughing, and having a ridiculous amount of fun. They were compassionate, but they could also speak the truth. These ladies were radiant.

Chloe was another woman who pointed my young heart to Jesus's grace. Chloe was an opera singer with beautiful red hair and a fiery personality. She had two baby girls and a husband who loved her. The two of them led our youth group for a while. They opened their home to us crazy kids, feeding us so much food and making us feel right at home. They brought us into their lives, and their lives weren't perfect.

They never tried to pretend. They never made us believe things were perfect when they weren't. They just loved Jesus and brought us in. Their door was open, and trust me, we teenagers took advantage of that. They had to deal with hormonal youngsters, and they did so with patience.

Jesus was a part of Chloe's life, and what poured out was God's amazing grace. Because she wasn't perfect, kids could relate to her. We felt comfortable and open with her.

She never acted "too much above us." She was real, and she was the mentor we needed.

Just in case you think all the grace people I know are women, I want to introduce to you three men who have shown me glimpses of Jesus's kindness.

When I think about the first guy, I picture a simply dressed, bearded fellow with kind eyes and a can of coke in hand.

Growing up, Joe was a rebel. I would hear stories about his crazy days as a young guy. He was probably the "biker type." He probably wore a leather jacket, had shaggy hair, and listened to loud music. In a Bible belt of a town, everyone probably knew about him, remembering him at prayer meetings, and hoping that he would turn his life around. I remember hearing about a motorcycle accident he'd had when he was younger. Joe was a rebel, a wild guy.

But I never knew that Joe. I'll tell you about the Joe I knew.

The Joe I knew wasn't a rebel. He wasn't a wild teenager people worried about. He was my youth pastor and the kindest guy you'd ever seen.

Pastor Joe was quiet and soft-spoken. When he would preach on Sundays, his sermons were three points and practical. He was gentle and wise. He didn't overcomplicate life or faith.

And he still loved driving fast. He had a cool car that was the closest thing to a race car I'd ever been in. It was old and not what you'd call flashy, but it was a blast. My friends and I, including a few of his daughters, would pile into his backseat like sardines. He would take us for a spin, doing donuts in the church parking lot. At a time when I was experiencing a lot of changes that come with growing up, Pastor Joe was a fun and steady pillar in my life.

When I think of Pastor Joe, I think of a guy with a ginormous heart. To him, the Christian life wasn't a set of dos and don'ts, nor was it just theological principles people could debate. It was just true, and it turned a wild rebel into a kind pastor with a cool car—a grace guy who showed me kindness I won't forget.

The second guy is also a *grace guy*.

This man has a big heart for God, reaching the lost, and working in business. He is intelligent, warm, and genuine, but he also struggles. At times, he has felt so passionate about sharing the good news and carrying a burden for the lost that he feels paralyzed by fear and indecision. He has been overcome with wanting to follow God but struggles to know what that means. While his heart is tender, he sometimes struggles to find peace.

But when I think about *my dad*, I think of a guy who loves Jesus and walks with Him. I think of a guy who is imperfect yet purely loves his family. I think of a guy whom I have always respected—who shows me what it means to be faithful but still struggle.

I don't think my dad is naturally a grace person. He's an achiever who wants to please his parents and tends to think he can take the world on his shoulders.

But when Jesus touches him, when he experiences God's grace, my dad is at rest. He is full of joy and excitement over life, and this fellow struggler can look me in the eye and say, "It's time to relax."

The last guy I want to share about was neither put together nor promising. When his wife met him, her successful career-filled life couldn't have looked more different than his. People were perplexed when they saw them going out. "What is she thinking?" they might have asked.

But despite William's rough beginnings, God used him in amazing ways. William served as a pastor for years. He is probably the favourite substitute teacher for many kids. He helps his wife minister to broken women by leading a Bible study and church service for them. As I've gotten to know William, I've seen a guy with a big smile, a loud personality, and a grace-filled heart. William loves people.

He cares for them and makes them smile. He nagged me to come to their house for several months until I finally did. I felt so cared for and welcomed by them. When I was going away for Christmas, William hugged me. When I was having a bad day, William noticed and asked about it.

William is a *grace guy*.

GRACE PEOPLE

Some were rebels through and through.
And still, they fight the status quo.
But that same fire that stoked their hate.
Now warms their heart and makes love grow.
Some were Pharisees, driven by guilt.
Their heart condemned; their minds obsessed.
They acted good yet knew they weren't.
But now He's freed them and given them rest.
Some are children who know they're loved.
Some like race cars and coffee mugs.
Some might fill the room with laughter.
Some run races or give good hugs.
But they've been changed by one great Saviour.
They no longer try to prove.
They know they're loved, fully accepted
For Grace Himself has made them new.

PRAYER

God, thank you for showing me glimpses of your heart. Thank you that you can take the most broken, fearful, legalistic, or defiant person and make them someone altogether new. Continue to change me. Make me a grace person, and use me in others' lives as you've used people in mine to showcase and proclaim your undeserved kindness.

GRACE LEADS TO SELFLESSNESS

CHAPTER TWELVE

I'm used to people looking at me. They look up to me, esteem me, and want to be like me. No one questions my integrity, wisdom, or commitment. I look great on the outside, and people like me. I have a lot to offer people and the world. I'm talented and smart, and people call me wise.

I live by many rules, so much so that when I do anything even mildly incorrect or not in keeping with my strict code of conduct, I feel condemned. I might get robbed of sleep, appetite, confidence, logical thinking, and for sure peace. I try to do the right thing—always. I try to love Jesus—always. And yet, I always feel as though I'm lacking. I always feel burnt out and tired, like I'm never good enough.

I invited Jesus to my house today, making sure everything was ready. I gave Him the seat of honour and offered Him the best meat, wine, and entertainment possible. Everyone would know how much I love Jesus, and more importantly, I would know. I'd finally be able to rest easy, knowing that I'd met the standard and loved Jesus perfectly. I would no longer question my commitment. I would have done it.

But something terrible happened, something from which I still haven't recovered. I'm struggling to understand what was done and said.

As we were eating, a woman came in—you know the one, everyone talks about her. You can spot her a mile away because everyone clears the road. You can smell her from a distance because she wears so much perfume it's suffocating. She hangs out with the bad crowd (she is the bad crowd). I wouldn't be caught dead talking to her.

But someone let her in, and there she stood. She approached Jesus before I could stop her. "Who let this woman in?" I asked. I was going to motion to my servant to get her out when she suddenly knelt beside Jesus, washing his feet. But she didn't use water from a basin—she used her tears. She didn't use a towel to dry. She used her hair. She carried a bottle of perfume, probably the stuff she bathes in. It must have cost a fortune. She bent down farther and started kissing Jesus's feet—yes, kissing them. Suddenly, she opened the bottle, pouring it on His feet—every drop. The smell was sickly sweet, and I began to cough.

I was overwhelmed. Who was this Jesus? Is He even a prophet like people say? Why is He letting this woman touch Him? Does he know who she is?

Before I could wonder more, I heard Jesus say my name. "Simon," he said. "I have something to say to you."

I sat up straighter. "Yes?"

GRACE LEADS TO SELFLESSNESS

"There was a man who loaned money to two people. He lent five hundred pieces of silver to one and fifty pieces of silver to the other."

"I don't owe any debts at all," I whispered to myself, hoping someone else would hear.

"Neither could pay their debts. Neither had enough money."

"How irresponsible. What carelessness!"

"So the man kindly forgave the debts of both. Who do you think loved him more?"

I thought quickly. What was Jesus getting at? The obvious answer, the most logical one, would be the one who owed him more. "I suppose the one who owed him more," I replied.

"That's right," Jesus answered.

I felt satisfied I had answered the question correctly, but then Jesus turned to face the woman... the sinful woman, and things took a strange turn.

"Look at her, Simon. She loves me. You didn't offer me water to wash my feet, but she has bathed them with her tears and wiped them with her hair. She loves me.

"When I entered your home, you didn't greet me with a kiss, but she has not stopped kissing my feet. She loves me.

"You didn't give me olive oil to anoint my head, but she has blessed me with this expensive perfume. She loves me, Simon."

My mind raced. Was Jesus commending this woman rather than me? Had she caught something I hadn't?

"She has many, many sins, but I have forgiven her, so she has shown me much love. But a person who is forgiven little only loves a little."

Jesus is now looking at the woman... that sinful woman. His voice is now tender, and yet he speaks with such authority, "Your sins are forgiven."

A murmur goes around the table. What makes this man think he can forgive sins?

But Jesus keeps looking at the woman. He keeps speaking, "Your faith has saved you; go in peace."

I can hardly think. I watch the woman get up, dry her tears, and close her bottle. She understands something I don't. She gets it, and as I watch her leave, I know I want what she has.

Grace-*fullness* will lead to self-*lessness*. When I'm wrapped up in my head, obsessed with my sin, and believe I'm condemned, I can't care for others. My strength is sapped. Self-absorption has closed my heart to grace, leaving nothing but impatience for others.

My friend Marissa helped me see something. Being a fellow "good girl" and "rule follower," she explained, "Satan knows he probably won't get us to sleep around or steal. He knows that if he can get us trapped in our heads, he can make us ineffective."

Indeed, when I hold myself to an impossible standard, I become ineffective, trying through vain efforts to earn or keep my standing with Jesus—believing that the more sacrifices I make, the more God will love me. While being hard on myself, that is trying to earn God's grace, can look pious, it is pointless, powerless, and perilous.

Grace Leads to Selflessness

Being hard on ourselves is pointless because it's unnecessary. I don't need to be hard on myself because Jesus kept the law perfectly, and I'm united with Him; like a man and woman are united in marriage, everything that belongs to Jesus is given to me.

Being hard on ourselves is powerless. Sometimes I think that the harder I am on myself, the more loving I will be. I believe that the more I beat myself up, the more sacrificial and fruitful I will become. That is the opposite of the truth.

God loved us, forgave us, and has done so much for us—now, we love, forgive, and serve others. When we lose the first part, we don't have the power to do the second. It's only as I abide in Jesus (John 15) that He produces the fruit of love, joy, gentleness, etc., in my life (Galatians 5:22-23).

"And I am praying that you will put into action the generosity that comes from your faith as you understand and experience all the good things we have in Christ" (Philemon 1:6).

Did you catch that? Paul prayed that Philemon would be generous, which comes from faith as he understands and experiences what he has in Christ.

Being hard on ourselves is also perilous. When we lose sight of God's grace and strive to do it ourselves, we stumble over the stumbling stone. The Bible is clear: if we choose law over grace, we better be perfect. If we try to do it ourselves and mess up once, we are condemned.

And friend, we can't do it ourselves. We mess up not just once but over and over again. Why not entrust yourself to someone who *can* do it? Don't try to do it yourself. The cost is too great.

My friend Cassandra is a selfless person.

Cassandra and her husband were missionaries in South America for many years. They raised children there, and they often went without and lived outside their comfort zones. Cassandra does things big. She has a big family, makes big meals, and has a big heart. Having a big heart often causes her to worry, but her struggles don't stop her from serving. Her fears don't stop her from giving her life away. Cassandra opened up her heart and home to many, including me, for a few months when I lived with her family.

When I'm in Cassandra's home, I feel loved and at rest. Whether it's enjoying a cup of coffee in her kitchen, having a bath in her basement, napping on her couch, or peeling potatoes at her side, I feel cared for. Cassandra is beautiful, but her beauty is different than what you'd find on a billboard. She doesn't strive for a perfect body, perfect hair, perfect skin, or maintain a perfect image. Her beauty runs far deeper. It's a beauty that comes from giving her life away, and giving her life away isn't something she does under compulsion.

Often when I hear that phrase—giving your life away—I get afraid. I imagine a terrible life, a life of misery and darkness, but then I look at Cassandra. Her life is anything but miserable, anything but dark. Her life is full. She experiences the abundant life Jesus came to bring (John 10:10). Even though she worries, I can see her heart is at rest. Even though she struggles, I can see she is secure.

Out of that security, Cassandra loves. Because she's received grace, Cassandra gives it.

My friend Lydia is also a selfless person.

Lydia speaks openly about Jesus's love and care. Her words and her prayers are rich with reminders of God's compassion and tenderness. She is soft-spoken (and may I add, she has a great Ukrainian accent), gentle, and far from demanding. I've never heard her speak a harsh word against others or herself. I was talking to her the other day, and we were discussing spiritual warfare. She told me, "Felicia, you don't have to listen to the enemy. He has no business speaking to you, even if some of his words are true." She is gutsy about the truth, and the way she holds herself is indeed grace-*full*.

From what I've seen, Lydia isn't "hard on herself."

She believes in God's love for her (1 Jn. 4:16).

And what is the result? Does being graceful make her lazy? Does believing in God's love for her drive her to be selfish and proud?

Just the opposite.

Lydia is one of the most patient, hardworking and beautiful people I know. She is a caseworker for women with addictions, and as I work down the hall from her and hear the women calling her name, wanting her to make calls for them, answer their questions, and endlessly serve their needs, I find myself getting impatient. "They are so demanding," I think. "She never gets a break!"

How does Lydia respond? She never raises her voice. She never acts impatiently or complains. She works hard. She fights for these ladies. She helps them in meaningful, practical, and nitty-gritty ways. Lydia is an advocate, a friend, and a wise counsellor.

She also cares for me. I've had hard days, and Lydia's smile can remind me of God's grace. I was eating lunch the other day, and she briefly put her hand on me as she walked toward the salad bar. However, because I had shared my heart and been met with such grace, I felt God ministering through her. Lydia personifies a grace-*full* person, and she didn't get there by beating herself up.

Could it be that Satan tries to prevent us from resting in Jesus because he knows where it will lead? Could it be that he tries to keep us from believing in God's love so that we will remain ineffective ministers of the gospel?

Accepting God's grace—his undeserved kindness (Rom. 3:24)—doesn't lead to selfishness. Beating ourselves up does. Perhaps gracelessness is pride in disguise.

Let's not be deceived.

Let's accept God's grace and become selfless.

GRACE WAS A STRANGER

She followed the rules
No one could dispute
She kept every law
And wrote a few too.
She never talked back.
She never did lie.
Except to herself.
Oh, how she tried.
Since grace was a stranger.
She had no other choice.
But to be without flaw.
And lose all her joy.
She knew she must love.
And for love did she aim.
She knew she must care.
She took every pain.
But her efforts fell short.
And since law she did choose.
Because she miss-stepped.
She would in the end lose.
If only she'd known.
That He loved her first.
She had nothing to earn.
Nor her value to prove.
If she had but trusted.
In Him who was perfect.

> She could step off the tightrope.
> And stop trying to fake it.
> Only then would His love
> Begin to flow through
> Even she'd be amazed
> At the fruit He'd produce.

PRAYER

Jesus, thank you for all that you've done for me. Help me to love you and others because of how much you've loved me. Make me grace-*full*, so that I can be truly self-*less*.

LET HIM
LOVE YOU

CHAPTER THIRTEEN

"Let Him Love You." These are the words my mom once told me. I had been dating a boy for a little while, and I was smitten. He was intentional, kind, patient, and a gentleman. He loved Jesus, and he knew God's Word. He patterned his life after the truth, and he really pursued me.

I was smitten.

But I was also afraid.

I was afraid to let myself like him and be pursued by him. I was afraid of making a mistake.

Fear. Fear. And more fear.

I knew he liked me, and I liked him. Yet my fear was holding me back from really enjoying this gift.

One day, I called my parents and told them I was afraid.

My mom was kind but frank. "Felicia, all my life I have struggled with fear. When I was single, I feared that I would never get married. When I was married, I worried about our living situation. When I was a mom, I worried about my kids. There will always be something to fear, so tackle it now. Stop living in fear and start telling him how much you appreciate him. Be his biggest fan...

"Let him love you."

She hit the nail on the head.

I had been resisting because of fear, afraid that if I continued this relationship, one of us would make a mistake, and we'd be forced to part ways. I didn't believe there was any grace or forgiveness available. I thought that we had better do it perfectly if we were to do it at all.

I believed a lie.

A good man was pursuing me. He loved me, and I was running from it.

The problem was deeper than it appeared.

The problem was that I wasn't letting God love me. I resisted because I was so afraid of making a mistake, being condemned, and losing my relationship with Him. I didn't believe His grace. I believed, "Be perfect or else." I was so afraid of making a mistake because I thought that would be the end of it.

But it's not.

Jesus loves me.

And all I must do is open my heart.

This wonderful boy was pursuing me.

And all I had to do was open my hands.

As long as we try to be perfect, so we aren't condemned, we're not believing the gospel.

We may say: Jesus loved me when I was a sinner, and He forgives me when I sin.

But at the heart level, we believe: Jesus loves me only when I do right, and if I sin, all is lost.

But that isn't the gospel.

Let's look at our hearts. What are they believing? Are they resisting Jesus's love?

Or are our hearts resting in it? Are they beginning to fathom how deep and tall and wide His love is? Are they free in it? Free enough to dance? There's room.

Let's look at our hands. Are they closed? Are our knuckles white, attempting to be perfect and fearing we're not?

Or are they open? Are they receiving Christ's love and His good gifts? Are they open to let others in and share the love they have received?

The choice is yours. The choice is mine. Are we going to strive? Or receive? I don't know about you, but I've seen firsthand where striving leads. Striving doesn't produce good fruit. It cripples and confuses. I've also seen where receiving takes you. It takes you to peace, rest, and an abundant life that sacrificially lays itself down for others.

But it starts here. Don't overthink it.

Just make a choice.

Let Him love you.

LET HIM LOVE YOU

It's easy to work but hard to be loved.
It's easy to build but hard to break down.
Creating big walls makes us feel put together.
But when we are sought, we fear being found.
We know how to buy and sell and produce.
We know how to give, then boast in it too.
Then someone comes round and gives you their heart.
Then love becomes hard, and you fear all you'll lose.
He's giving you gifts; just reach out and take them.
Stop trying to earn, control, and construe.
While you have been running and worried and panicked.
He has been speaking, "Just Let Me Love You."

PRAYER

Father, from this moment forward, I'm going to open my heart and open my hands to receive your good gifts. I recognize I'll make mistakes, but thank you that there's even grace for that. I'm going to let you love me, and I'm going to let others love me too.

STOP WORKING

EPILOGUE

One day, two men go walking. They are walking in the same direction, and both approach the temple. In some ways, they are similar. They both profess to love God. They are both going to pray and know God's righteous rules, and they both desire to follow them. But, they are very different.

Two approach the temple.

The first is a Pharisee. His week has been spent meditating on the law. He has made spiritual goals for Himself and knocked them out of the park. He has fasted, sacrificing his comfort to pray. He has given his tithe, even though perhaps it was inconvenient, or he could have spent it elsewhere. He has tried to live a holy life without sin. He's had a good week. He's had victory! He stands and prays confidently. "Thank you that I'm better than them," he says.

The second is a tax collector. His week has been hard. He knows God's law, enough to know that he's failed. Even though he tries to do right, he keeps messing things up. "I can't do it," he whispers to himself. He's defrauded people. He's yelled at his wife. He's *neglected his children. Now, he's come to the temple—but barely has the nerve to draw near. He can't lift his eyes. Instead, he beats his chest, crying, "God, be merciful to me, a sinner!"*

He didn't work. He just called out for help.

Once upon a time, there was a young man. He lived with his mom, dad, and older brother. While his older brother always did what their dad wanted, he was different. He had a wild streak. One day, he went to his dad and asked for money. "Dad, remember all that money you put into my college fund? I need it now."

His dad was hesitant because he knew all too well that his son wasn't planning to attend Harvard. He knew that his son wanted some freedom, and he feared he would make unsafe choices. However, he also knew that he couldn't hold him back, so he went to the bank and withdrew the money. He gave it to his son, and in less than twenty-four hours, his son had gone.

Things didn't go as the son expected. Sure, he had fun at first, but soon he had spent all his money, and because he had no money left, he also had no friends. "Maybe I can get a job," he thought. He went online and found an ad. "Local Farmer In Need Of Help."

The young man sent in his resume and was quickly hired, but it turned out to be nothing like what he was expecting. He could hardly make ends meet. He was desperate. "I better go home," he said. "Maybe I could work for my dad... I wouldn't need much. I could even sleep in the barn."

So he gave his notice and headed home. All the way, he planned and rehearsed his lines. Maybe his dad would take him on for the summer.

But as he approached the house, he came within sight of his dad. He stopped, unsure. Maybe he should practice his lines one more time. He started rehearsing, but his dad seemed to be getting closer. His heart began to race. Was his dad running? "Quick!" the boy told himself. "What were you going to say? I can't even remember the first part!"

Before he knew it, his dad was there, right in front of him, breathless.

The boy tried to think of what he'd planned to say. He tried to recite his perfectly planned apology, but nothing came out. He sputtered a few words before his dad interrupted. His dad had always said not to interrupt, but here he was doing it himself.

The boy listened, realizing his dad wasn't even talking to him. He was calling his staff. "Put on the roast! Get out the china! He's back! My son's back! Oh, and take my card to the store and buy him some new clothes. He's filthy!"

The boy was speechless. Nothing had gone as planned. He hadn't even gotten the words out. He hadn't even made it into the farmyard. He hadn't been planning on even living in the house, much less getting new clothes and a dinner party.

He didn't work. He just went home.

Friend, I have written pages about gracelessness and gracefulness. I have described people who characterize grace and told stories. Hopefully, I have inspired you and shown you the truth of the gospel, that God loves you. He doesn't give us what we deserve. Rather, in mercy, He gives us the very thing we don't deserve. He gives us hope. While we deserve condemnation, He gives us hope. We could never earn it, and we can never pay Him back. That's grace.

Now what? What do we do with all of this? How do we live in light of grace?

I want to propose to you one thing, one takeaway.

As you close this book, here's my challenge to you, and it's going to seem counter-intuitive: *Stop working.*

"And to the one who does not work but believes in Him who justifies the ungodly, his faith is counted as righteousness" (Romans 4:5 ESV).

Those who don't believe in God's gracious gift of salvation *work*. They work to be accepted, feel accepted, and stay accepted. They work to pay Jesus back—as if that were even possible. They work to make themselves perfect. They work to silence the accusing voice inside and ease their guilt.

On the flip side, those who believe in God's gracious gift of salvation *don't work*. They don't try to perfect their image or earn their place in God's family. They don't strive to save or sanctify themselves. Rather, they trust that Jesus's salvation accomplishes those things, and they know it's all been freely given.

The choice is yours. Who do you want to be today? Who do you want to be in five, ten, or twenty years?

When people look at you, what do you want them to say? How do you want them to describe you?

Now contrast those words with what you strive for every day. While many of us admire grace people, we strive to be something different. While we want to be gracious, rooted, and empathetic, we often spend our energy trying to be perfect while turning into a Pharisee.

What's exciting is that we can start today. We can make a choice right now to go a different way. What will you choose?

PRAYER

> Jesus, I'm ready to stop working. I'm ready to trust that what you've done is enough. I'm ready to rest and be transformed by your amazing grace.

www.ingramcontent.com/pod-product-compliance
Lightning Source LLC
Chambersburg PA
CBHW062114080426
42734CB00012B/2863